This book is dedicated to all who find Nature not an adversary to conquer and destroy, but a storehouse of infinite knowledge and experience linking man to all things past and present. They know conserving the natural environment is essential to our future well-being.

GLACIER
THE STORY BEHIND THE SCENERY®

by Kathleen E. Ahlenslager

Kathy Ahlenslager has worked as a summer naturalist at Glacier National Park since 1978. She graduated from the University of California, Santa Barbara, in environmental studies and geography. Kathy has a master's degree in botany from the University of Montana, where she works as a botanist during winter months.

Front cover: St. Mary Lake at sunrise; and Inside front cover: Beargrass and Mount Reynolds; photos by Jeff Gnass. Title page: Mountain goat; photo by Larry Burton. Pages 2/3: Citadel Mountain and Heavy Runner Mountain; photo by Larry Ulrich.

Edited by Mary Lu Moore, Book Design by K. C. DenDooven

GLACIER: THE STORY BEHIND THE SCENERY. © 1988 KC PUBLICATIONS, INC.
LC 88-080118. ISBN 0-88714-018-1.

The glaciated landscape of rugged mountains and deep valleys speaks of past millenia. The dynamic processes that have shaped the land continue to do so, while numerous plants and animals take up their places on its surface. Glacier National Park is a celebration of life and its never-ending cycles.

Glacier National Park is characterized by alpine glaciers, turquoise lakes, and Rocky Mountain wildlife. Throughout the park rugged mountain peaks rise far above rounded valleys, the work of Ice Age glaciers. Over 700 miles of hiking trails traverse glacially sculptured U-shaped valleys, horn-shaped peaks, and sheer-walled basins.

Backbone of the park, the jagged crest of the Continental Divide splits Glacier into two climatic regions. West of the Divide, Pacific fronts bring heavy precipitation and moderate temperatures.

To the east, dry continental air coupled with desiccating winds creates a colder, more severe environment. Weather patterns and topography have come together in Glacier to create a land of sharp contrasts and diversity.

Moist areas west of the divide give rise to cedar-hemlock forests; spruce-fir forests cover drier slopes. Vivid alpine meadows spread over the high country, and rich prairies reach into the plains. Grizzly bears and wolves, symbols of wilderness, roam free on this landscape, along with

black bears, bighorn sheep, and mountain goats. Glacier is a refuge for these and many other indigenous animal species.

The 49th parallel separates the United States and Canada on paper, but it does not delineate distributions of plants, animals, or rock formations. The park is not only a meeting place for plants and wildlife but also for people. Glacier's neighboring Canadian sister is Waterton Lakes National Park. Together these two parks are Waterton-Glacier International Peace Park, the first of its kind commemorating peace and goodwill between two countries. In a world of shared resources this International Peace Park symbolizes the need for cooperation and stewardship among all peoples.

Glacier National Park is a rugged and diverse land, yet it is also a fragile wilderness. This is the story of that land, one of the largest intact wild areas in the United States.

Mud to Mountains

Glacier is a geologic park. The mountainous landscape consists of uplifted and glaciated sedimentary rocks that are over one billion years old. These colorful rock layers are some of the oldest and, for their age, best preserved sedimentary rocks in the United States. Ice Age glaciers cut through this terrain and exposed the strata, layered like a cut deck of cards. Two parallel mountain ranges traverse it, trending from northwest to southeast. The Contintental Divide follows the Lewis Range through the center of the park, with the Livingston Range lying to the west. Elevations vary from 3,000 feet near Lake McDonald to 10,466-foot Mount Cleveland.

A Dynamic Earth

The interaction of water, land, climate, and various life forms operates through a variety of never-ending cycles to change the landscape. Erosion and weathering take place very slowly; earthquakes, volcanoes, landslides, and floods can quickly and dramatically alter terrain, however. All of these are reminders that our planet is a dynamic system in which mountains are constantly being uplifted and worn down.

The earth's surface is broken up into more than 20 plates, similar to the cracked shell around a hard-boiled egg. These plates, several hundred miles thick, float and move on softer, more pliable rocks below them in the earth's mantle. The plates, carrying the continents on them, shift and collide with one another due to convective currents within the hot, pliable mantle.

DAVID MUENCH

Following the deposition and compression of sediments into rock, the surface of the earth was uplifted. Ice Age glaciers sculptured a high plateau of rolling hills into the familiar rugged landscape of today. Backbone of the park, the Continental Divide towers above Hidden Lake. The surface of the land continues to change as erosion wears down the mountains.

Over half a billion years of deposition of sand, silt, and carbonate mud in a shallow sea are recorded in these rock layers. Buried sediments were compacted and cemented together by the weight of overlying layers. The types of rocks formed changed with climate, water depth, and kind of sediment.

KATHLEEN AHLENSLAGER

Ripple marks in rock are a reminder of ancient times when shallow water currents moved across tidal mudflats. Once covered by successive layers of fine-grained sediments, mud ripples are again exposed as erosion peels away millions of years of overlying rock layers. The characteristic red rock of the Grinnell Formation contains the iron-bearing mineral hematite.

An Ancient Sea

The North American continent of today is the result of the continuing motion of the earth's crust and continents. The most recent major episode occurred over 300 million years ago when the continents were joined together in a supercontinent, Pangea. Through movement of the earth's plates, referred to as *rifting*, Pangea broke up.

Slowly, over millions of years, the North American Plate rotated counterclockwise and drifted in a northwesterly direction to its present position. As this continental plate shifted, sediments and other continental fragments accumulated along the western margin, resulting in the present configuration of the western part of North America.

This type of plate movement has been occurring for at least two to three billion years of the earth's 4.5 billion-year life. Geologists think that in the distant geologic past North America was joined to Siberia. Beginning about 1.5 billion years ago, in a time period called the *Proterozoic*, this landmass began to break up along what is today the Rocky Mountain region. The ocean invaded this rift. Sediments, eroded from the neighboring highland areas, were deposited for over a half billion years along the margin of this ancient North American continent in the Belt Sea. Many tens of thousands of feet of sediment accumulated along the shallow continental margin. These sediments were then compacted and cemented to form the colorful rocks of western Montana and the Glacier region. Changes in climate, water depth, and in size and availability of the sediment particles resulted in the various rock types visible today.

Deposits of sand, silt, and carbonate mud were buried, compressed by their own weight; they cemented to form sandstone, siltstone, shale, limestone, and dolomite. The deeply buried sedi-

GEOLOGIC CROSS SECTION

Quaternary and Cretaceous formations

Tertiary: Kishenen Formation

Proterozoic:
Shepard Formation

Snowslip Formation

Helena (Siyeh) Formation and igneous sill

Empire Formation

Grinnell Formation

Appekunny Formation

Altyn Formation

Prichard Formation

Normal fault—*Arrows indicate direction of movement*

Thrust fault—*Arrow indicates direction of movement of upper plate*

This cross section of rock layers shows the formations seen in a straight line from Lake McDonald in the southwest to St. Mary at Glacier's east entrance. Mount Reynolds is along the Continental Divide near Logan Pass.

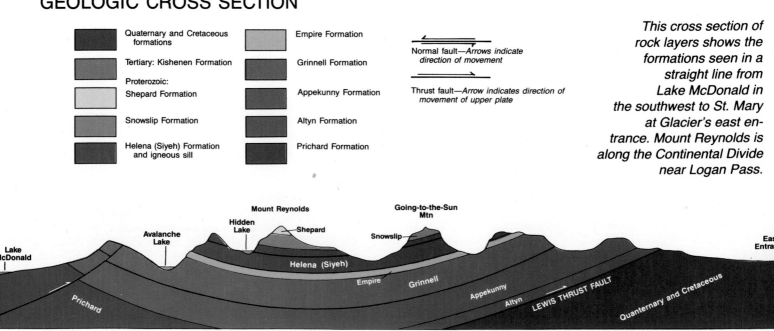

Glaciers dramatically changed the landscape two to three million years ago during the Pleistocene, or Ice Age. Although these rivers of ice are gone, the erosive power of water continues to alter the shapes of mountains and valleys. Water washing over mountains carries along everything from tiny soil particles to huge boulders.

ments experienced heat and pressure. Minerals in them were changed, or *metamorphosed*. Thus, sedimentary rocks were converted to quartzite, siltite, argillite, and recrystallized limestone and dolomite.

The Proterozoic Prichard and Altyn formations are the oldest rock layers of the Belt Sea series. The Prichard Formation is exposed on the west side of the park, and the Altyn Formation occurs on the east side. As these two are considered to be of similar age, it appears that their difference results from the westerly slope of the ancient Belt Sea floor.

Fine sediments composing the tan dolomite and limestone of the 1,400-foot-thick Altyn Formation were deposited in a warm, shallow sea. The weight of thousands of feet of these sediments deepened and warped the sea bottom. Consequently, both the Prichard and Altyn formations are overlain by the greenish-gray siltite and argillite of the 2,700-foot-thick Appekunny Formation. The color of this formation is from iron in a chemically reduced state, which was later incorporated in the micalike mineral chlorite.

GEOLOGIC TIME SCALE

EON	ERA	PERIOD	MILLIONS OF YEARS BEFORE PRESENT
	Cenozoic	Quaternary	2
		Tertiary	
			63
	Mesozoic	Cretaceous	138
		Jurassic	205
		Triassic	
			240
Phanerozoic		Permian	290
		Pennsylvanian	330
	Paleozoic	Mississippian	360
		Devonian	410
		Silurian	435
		Ordovician	500
		Cambrian	
			570
	Late		800
Proterozoic	Middle		1600
	Early		
			2500
	Late		3000
Archean	Middle		3400
	Early		3800
	pre-Archean		4550

The geologic history of the earth is divided into periods of time. The major divisions, eons, are in the left column of the scale. These are followed at the right by smaller divisions of time: eras and periods. The fourth column lists the number of millions of years before present.

The earth's geologic history extends to 4,550 million, or 4.5 billion years before present. At this time there were only simple forms of life. Thus the only known fossils in Glacier are blue-green algae. The Paleozoic Era is represented by the presence of animals with shells. Fish developed in the Silurian Period, amphibians in the Devonian, and reptiles in the Pennsylvanian. Dinosaurs flourished in the Mesozoic Era. Small mammals and birds appear in the Jurassic Period. Flowering plants date back to the Cretaceous Period.

As sediments accumulated, the sea gradually became shallower, and a broad tidal flat or other type of shallow-water environment developed. Fine-grained sediments deposited in shallow oxygen-rich water later formed the bright red Grinnell Formation. Evidence of current-formed ripple marks is preserved in the wavy surfaces of some rock planes. Mud cracks from periodic drying of the sediments also endure in this rock unit. In the 1,400-foot-thick Grinnell Formation the iron is in an oxidized state and is incorporated in the mineral hematite. Just a three-percent content of iron in these rocks is enough to color them a gaudy red.

Over millions of years the depositional environment of the Belt Sea slowly changed, and the sea bottom began subsiding again. During this transitional time the accumulation of sand, silt, and mud diminished, and the precipitation of calcium and magnesium carbonate minerals in the water increased. These materials were compressed and cemented to form the 800-foot-thick Empire Formation. This rock unit consists of calcium carbonate–rich green and red argillite, gray siltite, and white quartzite.

The colorful Empire Formation gives way to the gray and buff of the 3,000-foot-thick Siyeh Formation. This is the major cliff-forming unit in the park. It is composed of extremely resistant, chemically precipitated gray dolomite and limestone. Common within the Siyeh Formation are the growth patterns of ancient fossils of blue-green algae called *stromatolites*. These primitive plants are the only recorded life in the sea of that time. If other organisms lived in these waters, they left no recognizable evidence. Similar in structure to algae of today, the ancient algae took in carbon dioxide and released oxygen through the process of *photosynthesis*. Removal of carbon dioxide from the seawater triggered a chemical reac-

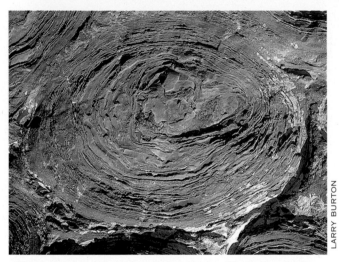

Concentric circles of limestone in the Siyeh Formation show the growth pattern of blue-green algae that grew in colonies in shallow areas of the Belt Sea.

The algae have decomposed and vanished. All that is left are the rounded patterns, or "cabbage heads," of the colonies. These are preserved in the gray rock of the Siyeh Formation, which weathers to a buff color.

A black band of igneous rock can be seen throughout Glacier. It formed as molten magma squeezed up through cracks in the floor of the Belt Sea and spread out between two layers in the Siyeh Formation. Mount Siyeh is one of six peaks in Glacier over 10,000 feet in elevation.

tion in which calcium carbonate particles precipitated out of the water, forming limestone.

As these particles precipitated they covered and killed parts of the ancient algal colonies. However, the sticky algal mats persisted and trapped the limestone particles along with mud and silt. The algal colonies had distinctive forms. Single colonies appear as cabbage shapes, while stacked colonies resemble single or branched columns.

A striking black band of igneous rock or *sill*, runs parallel with the carbonate layers in the Siyeh Formation. In some areas of the park the sill reaches a thickness of 300 feet. It has an average width of 100 feet—the height of a ten-story building. The sill is composed of an iron-rich rock known as *gabbro*. During deposition of the Siyeh Formation, this molten rock was injected into the sedimentary layers through cracks in the ancient sea floor. Other sills in the Siyeh Formation similar to the one found in Glacier have been dated at almost one billion years.

The depositional environment of the Snowslip Formation, which overlies the Siyeh Formation, was similar to the tidal flats in which the older Grinnell Formation sediments were deposited. Again, fine-grained sediments such as sands and silts accumulated on a subsiding sea floor. Besides green and red iron-bearing argillite and siltite, this colorful 1,800-foot-thick unit also contains crossbedded sandstone.

The youngest of the ancient Proterozoic rocks visible in the park is the dolomite and siltite Shepard Formation. Most of this rock unit has been eroded away, so that it is present on only a few of the high mountain peaks in the central and northern portions of the park.

Following this long, almost continuous period of sediment deposition that resulted in formation of the Belt Sea rocks, the region was alternately uplifted and submerged below sea level. From 570 to 240 million years ago, during the Paleozoic Era, limestone sediments were deposited in shallow seas over the Proterozoic rocks. In the Cretaceous Period of the Mesozoic Era, from 100 to 71 million years ago, the area of present-day Glacier National Park was again inundated by shallow seas in which mudstone and sandstone sediments were deposited.

MOUNTAINS ON THE MOVE

As the earth's plates separate, lava squeezes up to seal cracks in the ridges of the sea floor. Oceanic crustal plates form from basalt lava and are heavier than continental plates. Thus, when an oceanic plate collides with a continental plate, the heavier oceanic material usually sinks under the lighter continental plate in a process known as *subduction*.

About 150 million years ago the continental North American Plate and the oceanic plate lying to the west of North America started to move toward each other. As the heavier oceanic plate dipped down beneath the lighter continental plate the western edge of the North American Plate was elevated; volcanoes erupted as the subducted oceanic plate melted.

Compressional forces exerted during this time were so great that a fold slowly developed in the earth's crust west of today's Glacier National Park region. Over tens of millions of years, continuing pressures caused a great slab of crust to buckle, break, and finally, slide as a unit. This mass of rock, several hundred miles wide and at least 15,000 feet thick, slid over 50 miles from west to east. These rock layers slid like a tilted stack of pancakes, with some layers sliding more rapidly than others. During this period of uplifting and thrusting, weaker rock units were folded and deformed as they moved along a break in the rocks called the Lewis Thrust Fault.

The Lewis Fault is the major geologic feature in Glacier. The fault extends south of the park for over a hundred miles and north of it for several hundred miles. Because of the overthrusting of sedimentary rock layers, older Proterozoic rocks are superimposed over younger Cretaceous rocks. This is the reverse of the normal sequence, in which older rocks are overlain by younger ones.

As this huge slab of rock thrusted eastward, a downward warping of the rock layers, a *syncline*, developed. Today this can best be seen along Going-to-the-Sun Road west of Logan Pass. Rock layers to the west on Heaven's Peak slope down-

LARRY BURTON

ward to the east, and those of Haystack Butte to the east, slope downward to the west. On a larger scale, sedimentary layering seen throughout the park is like a canoe aligned to the north-south trend of the mountain ranges, the prow dipping down to the north and the sides dipping toward the middle of the canoe.

Natural forces on earth are always seeking balance. Even as the mountains of the Rockies were being uplifted, the combined erosional forces of water, wind, and gravity were lowering the surface of this high plateau. After the last invasion of the sea, the climate in the region was dry for several million years.

Thousands of feet of eroded rock and soil accumulated in valleys because there was insufficient water to form powerful enough streams and rivers to carry these materials away. Thus, erosion lowered and rounded the mountains. A high, rolling topography existed when glaciation began.

Rivers of Ice

For almost three million years, ice was the major erosional agent active in changing the landscape. A combination of factors produced a change in the climate from warm and dry to increasingly colder and wetter. Snow and ice accumulated on the continents and in the high mountains around

Ten miles long and about 300 feet deep, St. Mary Lake is one of the largest of the 650 lakes in Glacier. It was carved by Ice Age glaciers moving downslope off the northwest- to southeast-trending Continental Divide. These glaciers filled narrow, crooked stream-cut valleys. Pulled by gravity, these conveyor belts of ice transported rock downslope. In doing so they straightened and widened the valleys. After the retreat of these glaciers, water filled depressions in the U-shaped valleys. Several long finger lakes extend east and west from the Continental Divide. Loose accumulations of glacially transported rock debris, or moraines, dam many lakes in the park.

The gray glacial ice of Jackson Glacier contrasts with white snow left from the previous winter. Cracks in the ice, called crevasses, open from the downslope movement of the glacier and generally form perpendicular to the direction of glacial movement.

the world during this period called the Pleistocene, or Ice Age. Even though the Ice Age glaciers have retreated—most recently about 10,000 years ago—their effect on the terrain of Glacier is everywhere.

Continental ice sheets spread down from the north over much of North America but did not cover the area of Glacier. As the climate cooled, high alpine snowfields gave rise to massive rivers of ice that flowed down existing stream valleys. At least four major glacial advances and retreats, as well as numerous minor ones, slowly sculpted the spectacular scenery of Glacier. These glaciers reached their most recent maximum extent about 20,000 years ago, when the thickness of ice in some valleys was as much as 3,000 feet.

Glacial ice forms slowly as successive layers of light, fluffy snowflakes accumulate and aggregate with alternating freezing and melting to form granular ice. As these layers build up, the underlying granular ice recrystallizes, becomes denser, and eventually forms a massive sheet of ice. When enough ice finally accumulates on a slope, it slides of its own weight, forming a glacier.

Although ice cubes removed from a freezer are brittle and hard, the ice of glaciers becomes pliable, or plastic, from the massive weight of the overlying ice. The lower layers of ice exhibit a plastic flow very similar to tar, whereas the upper layers react like a brittle material. Cracks referred to as *crevasses* open up in the brittle upper zone from the movement of the ice below.

As glaciers move they quarry and pluck away at the land surface on valley floors and sides. They also erode headward into mountainsides, carving steep valley headwalls called *cirques* (pronounced "serks"). While glacial ice flows downhill, a crevasse known as a *bergshrund* forms between the glacier and the rock headwall, where in summer, meltwater freezes and joins the glacier to the headwall. Pieces of the headwall rock are plucked away as the glacier continues to move.

Glaciers continually undercut their headwalls and deepen the valley floor over which they flow by shearing uneven surfaces. After the glacier occupying a valley melts away, the valley displays a steep U-shaped cross section. Glacial lakes, or *tarns,* often occupy upper cirque basins, where dramatic sheer headwall cliffs rise several thousand feet above the valley floor. Cracker and Iceberg lakes in the Many Glacier area have spectacular examples of headwalls rising over 3,000 feet.

The knife-edged ridge (aréte) of the Dragon's Tail is the result of Ice Age glaciers cutting from opposite directions along this section of the Continental Divide. Waters flowing from Hidden Lake, perched below the Dragon's Tail, and from sharp-peaked Mount Brown eventually join the Pacific Ocean. Waters draining to the east meander into the Atlantic Ocean.

Two alpine glaciers may pluck away at headwalls from opposite directions and create a low saddle between the facing cirques called a *col*. Logan Pass, which separates the St. Mary and Lake McDonald valleys, is an excellent example of a col. Another erosional feature formed by glaciers is an *arête* (ah·RET), French for "fish bone." It results from glaciers carving along a ridge from two different sides and leaving behind a narrow, jagged ridge of rock like the Garden Wall, north of Logan Pass.

Where several glaciers have eroded into the flank of a mountaintop from different sides, a steep mountain peak, or *horn*, results. Mount Reynolds, above Logan Pass, and Flinsch Peak, in Two Medicine Valley, are two such steep-sided

Melting snow and rain feed Young Man Lake, nestled in a gigantic amphitheater. This steep-walled basin, or cirque, was gouged out by Ice Age glaciers carving into the mountainside. Pyramid-shaped peaks like Flinsch Peak form when glaciers work on several sides of a mountain. Flinsch Peak stands along the Continental Divide in the Two Medicine area.

DAVID MUENCH

pyramid-shaped mountains. Triple Divide Peak, southwest of St. Mary, is a unique horn located on the Continental Divide in such a position that runoff waters ultimately flow into three oceans: the Pacific via the Columbia River and its tributary the Flathead River, the Atlantic via the Missouri–Mississippi River drainage, and the Arctic via the Saskatchewan River drainage and Hudson Bay.

As Pleistocene glaciers flowed down winding, narrow, and shallow stream valleys, they slowly broadened and straightened the valleys into the present long, straight, deep troughs that extend generally east and west from the Continental Divide. The Going-to-the-Sun Road follows two of these major glaciated troughs: the St. Mary and McDonald Creek valleys.

In addition to the massive rivers of ice that filled the main valleys, smaller glaciers flowed from tributary valleys on the mountainsides. These glaciers did not have as much mass to erode as deeply as the larger glaciers, so when

Red and yellow monkey-flowers mingle with moss along the north-south Hudson Bay Divide. The headwaters of Hudson Bay and the Gulf of Mexico both originate in the high country of Glacier.

The headwaters of the Columbia River system lie north of Glacier, in Canada. West of the Continental Divide, water from the smallest splash to the swiftest current has the potential of ending up in the Pacific Ocean.

Triple Divide Peak is uniquely positioned along a ridge of Split Mountain, south of St. Mary. Water from rainfall and snowmelt on Triple Divide Peak flows into the watersheds of three oceans: the Pacific, the Atlantic, and the Arctic.

the last of the Ice Age glaciers finally melted away, these tributary valleys were left as *hanging valleys* perched high above the main valley floor. Bird Woman Falls, seen from the Going-to-the-Sun Road west of Logan Pass, drops from a dramatic hanging valley.

When glaciers melt and can no longer carry the rock debris they have carved from their valleys, they deposit it in front or along their edges in ridges or mounds called *moraines*. This ice-deposited rock, or *glacial till*, consists of unsorted material of various sizes, ranging from fine clay, silt, and sand to gravels and huge boulders. Today, moraines from the Ice Age glaciers are recognized as rounded tree-covered ridges bordering and damming the larger west-side lakes, including McDonald, Logging, Bowman, and Kintla.

LAND OF THE SHINING MOUNTAINS

Glaciers, like weather barometers, are sensitive to any change in the earth's climate. With a warming of the climate, the last of the Ice Age glaciers in this area melted away between 10,000

Interesting forms of ice take shape at the edge of Sexton Glacier near Siyeh Pass. Similar to most of the glaciers in the park, this small glacier is perched above treeline on a rock-strewn northeast-facing slope.

and 20,000 years ago. Thus there were probably no glaciers within today's park boundaries for several thousand years. About A.D. 1300, the global climate cooled slightly, resulting in the renewed formation of small alpine glaciers.

The glaciers found in the park today are probably of recent origin and are not feeble remnants of the major Pleistocene rivers of ice. The 50 or so present-day glaciers appear to have reached their farthest advance about A.D. 1700 and since then have been retreating. They cling to north- and northeast-facing slopes, where steep headwalls shade them from the melting rays of afternoon sunlight.

As gravity pulls the glaciers downhill, they drag along embedded rocks and soil that abrade and polish smooth the underlying bedrock. Like sandpaper, glaciers slowly grind up bits of rock they carry into very fine rock powder, or "flour." These tiny rock particles are so light that, when

Interpretive hikes are led to Grinnell Glacier, one of the largest in the park. Separated by 500 feet, Salamander and Grinnell glaciers were joined prior to 1926. The present-day glaciers have retreated markedly in the last 100 years.

they are carried by meltwater streams into nearby lakes, they remain suspended. As they reflect and refract sunlight they impart a beautiful turquoise blue to the water. Water colored white from large quantities of rock flour is known as glacial milk.

The glaciers now remaining in the park are located at the heads of mountain valleys and are accessible by hiking trails. The three largest—Blackfoot, Grinnell, and Sperry—are each a long day's hike from their respective trailhead. Although hiking on glaciers may be attractive, such travel requires experience and extreme caution to avoid weak snow bridges that may hide crevasses up to 50 or 75 feet deep.

Glacier National Park is so named because of its classic glacially carved topography, as recorded by numerous erosional features. The beautiful mountainous scenery seen today is but one frame of a continually changing landscape. In concert with glaciers, landslides, rockfalls, and mudflows, hundreds of miles of clear, swiftly flowing waters are continuously altering the land of the shining mountains.

These scattered rocks absorb the sun's warmth and melt into glacial surfaces.

As Grinnell Glacier moves it carries fallen rocks from its headwall. At the toe of the glacier, rocks are deposited like people off an escalator. Openings appear where large ice chunks have broken away in the warm summer sun.

SUGGESTED READINGS

Alt, David D., and Donald W. Hyndman. *Rocks, Ice & Water: The Geology of Waterton-Glacier Park.* Missoula, Montana: Mountain Press Publishing Company, 1973.

Johnson, Arthur. "Grinnell and Sperry Glaciers, Glacier National Park, Montana: A Record of Vanishing Ice." *U.S. Geological Survey Professional Paper 1180.* Washington, D.C.: U.S. Government Printing Office, 1980.

Raup, Omer B., and others. *Geology Along Going-to-the-Sun Road, Glacier National Park, Montana.* West Glacier, Montana: U.S. Geological Survey, 1983.

A Mixing of Floras

As the last of the Ice Age glaciers retreated, seeds and spores from surrounding areas scattered and germinated on the bare land. Some of these species still survive here, but others have come and gone with changing climatic conditions.

More than 1,000 species of plants presently inhabit the one million acres of Glacier. They migrated in from all directions and include species common in the northern Rocky Mountains as well as those from other areas. Plants of the Great Plains are at the western edge of their ranges in Glacier, and others common in the Cascade and Coast mountains of western Washington and British Columbia are at the eastern edge of their distributions. Several arctic-alpine species reach their southernmost extensions in the park. The pattern of vegetation found in Glacier is shaped by climate, geology, and natural disturbances such as fires, floods, and avalanches.

TODAY'S CLIMATE

Glacier's climate is transitional. The Continental Divide is a weather barrier. Moist maritime fronts west of the Divide bring abundant rain and snowfall and relatively mild winter temperatures. In contrast, the continental climate east of the Divide is characterized by wind and dramatic winter temperature fluctuations.

The average annual precipitation from rain and melted snow varies from 80 to 100 inches along the high slopes of the Continental Divide to 20 to 30 inches along the lower edges of the park. January is usually the coldest month, with average maximum temperatures in valley areas between 25° and 27° Fahrenheit. In contrast, average minimum temperatures for the warmest month, July, are between 72° and 80° F. Although extreme summer highs may reach 95° to 105° F, arctic air can bring extreme lows in winter of −40° to −55° F.

FOREST MOSAICS

For thousands of years lightning-caused fires have been a normal part of plant succession in the Glacier area. Lightning often strikes the park during August and September, when forests are dry. Over 850 fires have burned in the park since 1920, resulting in intricate mosaics of forests, shrubfields, and grasslands.

Flowers abound in the open subalpine meadows at Logan Pass. Red Indian paintbrush and pink monkey-flowers, along with yellow arnicas and grounsels, all bloom in profusion along the Hanging Gardens.

TOM ALGIRE

Fall brings a light dusting of snow to Heaven's Peak, and of yellow to cottonwood leaves along Going-to-the-Sun Road.

JEFF GNASS

Ignited by lightning, flames light up slopes below Heaven's Peak. This 1967 fire swept over large areas of the Glacier and Garden walls. Numerous lightning strikes occur each year, but not all result in fires. The possibility of fire ignition is enhanced by dry soil and vegetation, high daytime temperatures, and low humidity. Fire plays a natural role in the establishment and maintenance of the diverse vegetation in Glacier.

JEFF GNASS

Evidence of fires persists in the area of "the Loop" along the Going-to-the-Sun Road, where the 1967 Garden Wall fire burned a spruce-fir forest. Dead tree trunks from this fire stand amid shrub-covered slopes. Along the southern boundary of the park, south-facing slopes are still sparsely vegetated following fires in 1929. For many years fires were suppressed in Glacier. The importance of fire in the natural cycles of these forests is now better understood, and controlled burning may be reintroduced to some areas of the park.

The vegetation of Glacier is well suited to recurring fires. For example, some lodgepole pine

Thirteen years after the 1967 Garden Wall fire, shrubs, cottonwoods, and snags dominate the open slopes. Mature western larch that survived the fire are golden with fall leaves.

populations require fire to melt resin that seals closed, or *serotinous*, cones. Some cones open the second year, but serotinous ones may remain closed, lying on the ground or hanging in trees for decades.

These trees thrive in the conditions left in the wake of a fire: open, sunlit areas and bare soil that is often poor in nutrients. As a lodgepole forest matures, the forest floor becomes increasingly shaded, favoring shade-tolerant species such as Engelmann spruce and subalpine fir. Lodgepole pines are dependent upon the recurrence of disturbances such as fires. These trees are short-lived; they usually do not exceed 100 years. In the absence of fire, the shade-tolerant spruce-fir forest eventually succeeds the lodgepole pine forest.

With the suppression of fire in Glacier, extensive forests of lodgepole pines have reached maturity, a condition ripe for the cyclic infestations of mountain pine beetles. Adults bore through the bark of mature trees and lay their eggs. After the larvae hatch, they feed on the living tissue of

A dense stand of mountain hemlocks provides ideal conditions for an undergrowth of moss in the moist forests near Lake McDonald.

Periodic infestations of mountain pine beetles are a natural part of the cycle of a lodgepole forest.

trees and girdle them. Because national parks preserve natural processes, dead trees are not harvested for timber. They eventually blow over and slowly decompose, returning nutrients to the soil.

Although vegetation is distributed continuously over the landscape, the range of an individual species is restricted by several factors. Few plants found on mountain peaks also grow in valley bottoms. The kinds of plants growing on a slope change gradually or abruptly as some species drop out and new ones appear. Those sharing similar growing conditions can generally be divided into orderly groups, similar to neighborhood communities.

Plant communities occur in life zones or belts along elevational and latitudinal gradients. Life zones observed on a 6,000-foot climb up one of Glacier's mountains would be similar to those occurring on an 1,800-mile trip from the park north to the Arctic Circle. The life zones in Glacier intergrade and are roughly divided into lowland semi-arid grasslands, low- to mid-elevational forests, subalpine scrub forests, and alpine tundra.

Overleaf: The steep walls of Grinnell Point separate the Grinnell and Swiftcurrent valleys. Six of the remaining 40 to 50 glaciers in the park are in this area. Photo by Dick Dietrich.

Grasslands and forest mingle on the western edge of Glacier along the North Fork of the Flathead River valley. A diverse array of tree species and heights indicate a complex fire history in this area. Fire is important in maintaining grasslands. With the suppression of fires, trees invade wetmeadow and prairie openings.

Grasslands and Parklands

Below 4,500 feet, periodic fires sustain grasslands. Because grasses grow from their joints and not from their tips, they resprout quickly after fires or grazing by animals. Over 100 species of grasses thrive in the park. Grasslands east of the Continental Divide are similar to the prairies of southeastern Alberta, Canada, and eastern Montana. Those grasslands west of the Divide have affinities with the Palouse grass communities of Washington, Oregon, and Idaho.

The lower mountain slopes east of the Continental Divide consist of rolling grassland and aspen-covered moraines. Throughout the year, severe winds from the mountains sweep eastward across this open country. Unless blanketed with snow, moisture and soil are carried off by drying winds averaging 13 to 15 miles per hour. Sudden warm chinook winds may gust to 100 mph, causing dramatic daily temperature extremes. A record temperature drop of 100 degrees (44° F to −56° F) took place in 24 hours at Browning, Montana, near East Glacier, in January 1916, when chinook conditions were replaced by cold arctic air.

Extending south from Canada, groves of quaking aspen are maintained by fires that burn competing shade-tolerant, less fire-resistant trees. Fires also prompt aspen trees to develop extensive root suckers, which are new trees. Douglas fir, lodgepole pine, Engelmann spruce, and limber pine invade these aspen communities.

Grasslands west of the Continental Divide exist as a series of prairies nestled in the North Fork Valley, a broad trough more than 30 miles long and ranging up to four miles wide. Numerous lightning fires have swept through this valley, preserving pockets of native Palouse prairie species. Lodgepole pine and aspen border the prairies, with ponderosa pine savannahs between them. Variations in soil moisture influence the balance between grassland and forest.

Through this valley flows the North Fork of the Flathead River. It is the western border of the park, while the Middle Fork River marks the southern boundary. These rivers slowly move across broad floodplains, and periodically they flood. Black cottonwoods, willows, and horsetails thrive in these disturbed areas. The vegetation slowly stabilizes the floodplains until the rivers flow back to reclaim them.

Forested Slopes

Evergreen forests cover all but the highest peaks and rocky slopes of Glacier. Nearly two-thirds of the park is forested with 19 species of trees. Although vegetation on the west side of the Continental Divide may initially appear as

uniformly forested slopes, a north-south moisture difference allows for a great diversity of plant life. Moist cedar-hemlock forests growing in the Lake McDonald valley cannot survive in the drier valleys to the north and are replaced there by open forests of ponderosa pine and Douglas fir.

Western redcedar and western hemlock forests occur in the southwestern area of the park, primarily between Avalanche Creek and the head of Lake McDonald. Prior to a fire in 1910, this forest was more widespread. Cedar-hemlock forests flourish at 3,200 to 3,500 feet altitude, but they are not able to survive winter temperatures just 500 feet higher.

Trees in the cedar-hemlock forest create a dense canopy that allows very little light to reach the forest floor. Occupying the understory are shade-tolerant plants that include western yew, queen's cup beadlily, and devil's club. Lush cushions of mosses and liverworts carpet the ground, while colorful assortments of mushrooms change with the seasons.

Western larch is a long-lived tree that invades the cedar-hemlock forest after a fire. Larch is a conifer, but it is not an evergreen. In the fall it sheds its needles and is responsible for bright

Water from melting snow on Mount Despair feeds a pond at the head of Park Creek. Thick forests carpeting the valley bottom stop abruptly at the base of the dry and rocky mountain slopes. Soil and water linger on the narrow ledges of the mountain and provide favorable growing conditions for a few hardy plant species.

golden hues on the mountainsides, along with the yellow leaves of deciduous black cottonwood, paper birch, and quaking aspen.

A transitional forest of Douglas fir occurs on both sides of the Continental Divide between low-elevation grasslands and spruce-fir forests. Douglas fir is not a true fir. Its cones hang downward and do not disintegrate at maturity. Cones of true firs are borne upright and disintegrate when seeds are released.

Above 4,000 feet, Engelmann spruce and subalpine fir forests blanket both sides of the Continental Divide and extend to treeline, where scrub forests of subalpine fir prevail. Among the numerous shrubs growing in the spruce-fir understory are huckleberries, gooseberries, thimbleberries, elderberries, and serviceberries.

The wood nymph inhabits moist forests.

Spring brings blue camas flowers to cover east-side grasslands.

Brown-eyed Susans grow on sunny, well-drained slopes.

Raindrops cling to the textured surfaces of ferns growing near Lake McDonald.

Eight species of violets bloom in Glacier.

Golden mushrooms and green lichen emerge through pine-needle litter on the forest floor.

28

Glacier's Colorful Flora

A glance at the colorful blossoms flowering in its meadows, forests, and grasslands gives only a hint of the diverse flora of Glacier National Park. Each plant species will flourish only under its own specific environmental conditions.

Explorer's gentian thrives on moist, rocky soils near treeline.

Bishops-cap is identified by white flowers and dome-shaped fruit.

The orange false dandelion grows in subalpine forests.

The patterned leaves of false hellebore are unusual.

Glacier lilies bloom in the melting snow of alpine meadows. Their small bulbs are eaten by grizzly bears.

29

Sky pilots are characteristic of high country. They grow on dry talus slopes. Because of the odor from their leaves they are also called skunk plant.

KATHLEEN AHLENSLAGER

Hundreds of beargrass blossoms form distinctive white plumes on Glacier's slopes. Named by explorers Lewis and Clark, beargrass flowers are eaten by deer, elk, bighorn sheep, and squirrels.

RUSS FINLEY

The deep green of forested slopes is often interrupted by the brighter green of shrubs growing in avalanche chutes. Avalanches occur in winter and spring as unstable melting snow gives way under gravity. Plunging snow sets up a tremendous wind in front of it that snaps off trees extending above the snow cover.

Beargrass—a lily and not a grass—flourishes throughout the forest zone and is the unofficial flower of the park. It flowers every five to seven years. Seen at low elevations in May, blooming plants follow summer up the slopes. By August the flowering has reached treeline.

THE HIGH COUNTRY

Above 6,000 feet the dense forest zone gives way to widely spaced islands of dwarfed trees and lush meadows. With snow lingering into July and 700 inches of annual snowfall, the growing season is a mere six weeks. Treeline, a narrow band at the upper limits of tree growth, fluctuates in elevation, reflecting variations in temperature, moisture, wind, and snow cover. In Glacier, treeline averages 7,000 feet, but it is lower on windswept ridges and passes such as Logan Pass, where it is about 6,600 feet.

Subalpine fir is the most common tree of the scrub forest, although Engelmann spruce, whitebark pine, and limber pine also survive here. In the northern Rocky Mountains whitebark pine is characteristic of treeline. It is often the first tree to invade alpine meadows and acts as the nucleus for the establishment of tree "islands."

Trees growing in islands provide protection for one another against battering winds and frigid temperatures. Wind-borne ice crystals often shear off the growing buds of a tree, so that branches grow only on the leeward side. On exposed slopes trees no longer grow erect but are stunted and twisted, forming a *krummholz* vegetation, usually no more than two feet high. Krummholz literally means crooked wood.

Although not common in Glacier, subalpine larch is the unofficial tree of the park. Its distribution in the northern Rockies is restricted to the highest elevations of tree growth, where it maintains its erect posture even on north-facing slopes. As a deciduous upper-treeline conifer, subalpine larch is unique in North America.

The arctic-alpine zone occurs above 7,000 feet. This vast treeless expanse covers nearly one quarter of the park. Glacier's alpine is a mosaic of several plant communities. These vary with moisture availability from wet alpine bogs, meadows, and rock ledges to sparsely vegetated and rocky slopes.

Plants of the alpine are usually perennials no more than four inches tall, although some grow to a foot in height. Heathers, avens, and willows are among the few woody species present. Full-grown dwarfed willows, scarcely six inches high, form thick mats. Dense growth enables plants to conserve moisture and heat in addition to trapping soil and seeds.

KEITH GUNNAR

The whitebark pine survives at the upper limits of tree growth. By harvesting and caching its seeds, Clark's nutcrackers are important in the dispersal of this pine species.

LARRY BURTON

Only a few inches high, arctic willows form dense mats in Glacier's alpine zone. Similar to other willows, individual plants are either male or female.

Slopes of loose rock, or *talus,* and year-round snowfields cap the high country. Rocky and desolate mountain summits over 8,000 feet support several hardy species. These aptly named alpines include sky pilot, stonecrop, alpine buttercup, limestone columbine, and woolly daisy.

Snowfields also support plant life. Some algae possess oils that enable them to survive in snow and ice. At times the microscopic cells of these algae become so dense that they color the snow. One such alga gives melting summer snowbanks a reddish color, thus the term "watermelon snow."

From snow-covered mountain peaks to dense coniferous forests and windblown grasslands, Glacier National Park supports a rich mosaic of vegetation.

SUGGESTED READINGS

ARNO, STEPHEN F., and RAMONA P. HAMMERLY. *Timberline: Mountain and Arctic Forest Frontiers.* Seattle, Washington: The Mountaineers, 1984.

DeBOLT, ANN, and PETER LESICA. "Alpine Plants of Glacier National Park." In *Rocky Mountain Alpines.* J. T. Williams, ed. Denver: The Denver Botanic Garden, 1986.

KUIJT, JOB. *A Flora of Waterton Lakes National Park.* Edmonton, Alberta, Canada: University of Alberta Press, 1982.

LESICA, PETER. *Checklist of Vascular Plants of Glacier National Park, Montana, U.S.A.* West Glacier, Montana: Glacier Natural History Association, 1985.

NELSON, ALAN G. *Wild Flowers of Glacier National Park.* Great Falls, Montana: Alan G. Nelson, 1970.

SHAW, RICHARD J., and DANNY ON. *Plants of Waterton-Glacier National Parks.* Missoula, Montana: Mountain Press Publishing Company, 1979.

An Abundance of Wildlife

From free-ranging grizzly bears to migrating bald eagles, the wildlife of Glacier is varied and fascinating. All of the 60 mammal species inhabiting the park are native. In addition, animal life in Glacier comprises over 200 bird species, five amphibian species, and two nonvenomous snakes. Two species of large mammals that previously lived in the area and no longer range within the park are the mountain bison and the woodland caribou.

There is no fence around the park, so animals pass back and forth between it and adjoining public and private lands. As a wildlife sanctuary Glacier is a corridor for migration in an international wilderness region. Although some animals have adapted to specific life zones, others may range through several as they forage for food or migrate. Glacier encompasses 1,500 square miles, thus most of Glacier's wildlife has room to roam.

Each of the creatures found in Glacier has physical adaptations and patterns of behavior that enable it to endure the climate. Mountain goats and elk, among other animals, are active throughout the year, but marmots and chipmunks hibernate. Other creatures, like many of the birds, are only summer residents.

Prior to 1932, predator-control rangers shot and trapped what were then considered "bad" animals. These "varmints" were thought to serve no useful purpose. They included the timber wolf, mountain lion, and badger. At the same time, the "good" animals, such as deer, elk, and bighorn sheep, were fed. Today the vital role of predators in the web of life is better understood, and no animals are fed.

All wildlife is protected within the park. As wild creatures they are wary of people, and their behavior is unpredictable. No matter how tame an animal may appear, none should be approached. Viewing animals in rugged terrain and dense forests requires patience. The time taken to scan open slopes for wildlife is often rewarded.

Prairie Life

Open grasslands offer little in the way of protection from weather. Animals that live in prairie communities have found numerous ways to cope with wind, drought, temperature fluctuations, and intense sunlight. Many of the activities of smaller animals take place underground, for mice, ground squirrels, and badgers find shelter in burrows. Some rodents, like the northern pocket gopher, are seldom seen and exist on a diet of underground insects, worms, and roots.

HANS WENDLER

Columbian ground squirrels rarely climb trees, but seek protection in an intricate series of burrows in the ground. They range throughout Glacier from low to high elevations.

Majestic in its stature, the mountain goat is a symbol of the high country. This cliff-dwelling animal develops a thick insulating coat of fur enabling it to endure winter storms.

STEVEN HOLT

Columbian ground squirrels range from prairies through forested slopes to the alpine. Individuals sit upright and send out shrill alarm whistles to give warning of danger to others living in the colony. Almost three-fourths of a squirrel's five-year life is spent in hibernation.

Coyotes, mountain lions, and wolves are the largest predators of the grasslands, and they range throughout the park. Mostly nocturnal, they are rarely sighted by park visitors. With the disappearance of wolves, grizzlies, and mountain lions, the range of the intelligent and social coyote has increased. The coyote is an opportunist that eats anything from berries to carrion.

AQUATIC CORRIDORS

Rain and meltwater from glaciers and snowfields feed more than 200 lakes in Glacier. As wa-

Along lower McDonald Creek hundreds of bald eagles converge in the fall to feed on spawning kokanee salmon. Their aerial maneuvers are fascinating to watch as agile adult eagles swoop over the creek, reach into it, and snatch salmon from the water. The eagles fly in from summer nesting grounds to the north, stop to feed along McDonald Creek, then continue south to wintering areas.

NEAL & MARY JANE MISHLER

MARK MILLER

ter flows over the ground, nutrients dissolve and are used by terrestrial and aquatic plants. Minute animals and insects feed on aquatic plants.

Fish living in the waters of Glacier comprise native species along with introduced ones. Many of the east-side drainages and high mountain lakes originally lacked fish. Thousands of lake, rainbow, eastern brook, and Yellowstone cutthroat trout were stocked until the mid-1960s. Of the 22 species of fish found in Glacier, six are introduced.

Now established, many of these introduced fish populations compete with native species that include westslope cutthroat trout, bull trout, and mountain whitefish. Some are also predators on the native species, and others interbreed with them. The distribution of westslope cutthroat trout has decreased dramatically due to interbreeding with the more common Yellowstone cutthroat trout and predation by introduced lake trout.

Stocking has dramatically changed the aquatic ecosystems of the park. Today Glacier's waters are managed so as to protect native fish populations. Although all other wildlife is protected within the park, the tradition of fishing is still maintained.

Bald eagles gather near Apgar each fall to feed on spawning Kokanee salmon, a freshwater form of the Pacific Coast sockeye salmon. In 1916 Kokanee salmon were stocked in Flathead Lake, 60 miles downstream from the park, and in Lake McDonald in the 1920s. Thousands of four-year-old salmon migrate up the Flathead River in the fall to spawn on the shallow gravel beds of lower McDonald Creek in Glacier. Within three weeks of spawning they die. The following spring their young hatch and migrate to Flathead Lake.

Migrating south from their summer nesting areas in western Canada, hundreds of eagles feed on spawning salmon for a few weeks each fall before moving southward to various wintering sites in the western United States. Each morning in predawn darkness, eagles fly in from night roosts and take their places along the creek to fish until nightfall. Adult eagles dot trees lining the creek. Swooping down, they pluck the foot-long one-pound fish from the water. Young eagles, not as adept at these aerial maneuvers, wade into shallow waters to nab sluggish salmon. Waterfowl, coyotes, and bears also scavenge for this high-protein energy source.

Curious birds, water ouzels are well adapted to life along fast-moving creeks. Having oily plumage and strong legs, ouzels can walk underwater,

STEVEN HOLT

The moose is the largest of the ungulates (hoofed animals). Velvet envelops and nourishes the developing antlers in the fall. Similar to deer and elk, moose shed their antlers each year. Like all wild animals, moose are unpredictable and should not be approached. Occasionally people are treed by a charging moose.

feeding on insect larvae and fish. These small birds are fascinating to watch as they dive into the swift current, feed, and resurface in the same area. Easily identified by the bobbing up and down of their bodies, they also are called water dippers.

Although potable water in the park has been treated, water taken directly from lakes and streams should not be ingested, for it may contain a microscopic animal called *Giardia lamblia*. This parasite flourishes in the intestines of a variety of animals. In humans it may cause extreme sickness and weight loss. Excreted, a giardia cyst may survive up to two months in cold water.

After an absence of 50 years, the gray, or timber, wolf again roams within Glacier. An effective predator-control program exterminated them from the park. Today the wolf is recognized as an important member in the web of life and is making a comeback in the park.

Amid the leaf litter, twigs, and small plants of the forest floor live numerous spiders and other invertebrates, in addition to birds and small mammals. Rather than build a web, camouflaged crab spiders match the color of flowers on which they await insect prey. Also on the forest floor are weasels, active mostly at night. With streamlined bodies and small heads, they are able to squeeze into small places in their relentless pursuit of mice, moles, and small birds.

Referred to as "fool's hens," grouse display an apparent lack of fear and stand their ground when approached. Camouflaged in brown, white, and gray, grouse avoid movement so as not to catch the eye of a predator. Three species of grouse inhabit Glacier. Spruce grouse are year-round residents of spruce-fir and lodgepole forests. Ruffed grouse, however, prefer deciduous forests, and blue grouse live primarily in the Douglas fir forest.

A rarely seen member of the weasel family, the fisher, feeds nocturnally on small mammals, birds, and fruits. It is one of the few predators that eats porcupines. Individuals live in forested areas, usually not far from water.

The slap of a beaver's tail is a familiar sound around lakes and ponds in the park. Beavers not only gnaw aspen and willow branches for food but also dam streams with them. By flooding lowlands, they create a wetland habitat that is attractive to moose, mink, and muskrats.

Moose forage in shallow waters. Although they winter on twigs and bark in valley bottoms, they follow the spring and summer snowmelt up drainages to feed on aquatic vegetation. Similar to other mammals that endure the winters of Glaier, moose have a thick coat of hollow guard hairs and a wooly underfur that traps warm air next to their skin.

LIFE IN THE UNDERSTORY

Glacier's forested slopes are a complex world of elusive flutterings, scurryings, and fleeting shapes hidden by foliage. The spiraling trills of Swainson's thrushes, the whistles of varied thrushes, and the chattering of red squirrels, give evidence of life in the shaded understory.

The forests of Glacier consist of several layers that intergrade: forest floor, shrub, small tree understories, and treetop canopies. From nectar-feeding hummingbirds hovering over flowers to porcupines hunched in trees stripping bark, each creature has a specific role in the forest.

Snowshoe hares feed on succulent vegetation in young, open forests. Seasonally camouflaged, the hare's brown summer coat turns white in winter. The Canada lynx hunts hares to the extent that the population dynamics of the two animals are intertwined and cyclic. Both are large-footed—an aid in traveling over snow. Rarely seen, both animals are nocturnal.

Tangles of shrubs and small trees provide cover for nesting birds. Many of the birds in Glacier's

NEAL & MARY JANE MISHLER

LARRY BURTON

Sporting a white coat in winter and a brown one in summer, the short-tailed weasel depends on camouflage so that it can sneak up on prey. This small carnivore is an expert mouser. Like that of its relative the mink, the fur of the short-tailed weasel, or ermine, is valuable. In the area of Glacier, several furbearers were once hunted for their valuable pelts. Now all animals within the park are protected.

forests are only part-time residents, taking advantage of summer insects and fall berries. Flycatchers, waxwings, and swifts catch flying insects on the wing; woodpeckers, nuthatches, and creepers, however, glean insects from tree trunks and branches.

In the trees, red squirrels harvest conifer cones and cache them for use during the winter. Red squirrels and chipmunks, active during daylight hours, cover the same areas that flying squirrels and mice do at night. They share a diet of insects and seeds and are hunted by pine martens and great-horned owls.

Forests provide cover for larger animals in the winter. But in the spring, foraging deer, elk, and bears are attracted to the soft-stemmed grasses of open prairies. The diets of grizzlies and black bears consist of over 90 percent vegetation. As opportunists they also search for insects, small mammals, and carrion. Grizzlies forage at low elevations in the spring, then move up to high meadows for the summer. Although Alaskan relatives of the grizzly may weigh over 1,000 pounds, the grizzlies of Glacier rarely exceed 400 pounds.

Unlike ground squirrels, marmots, and chipmunks, bears are not true hibernators. The metabolic processes of these small rodents are so reduced that they cannot readily be aroused out of

LARRY BURTON

Pine martens are easily distinguished from other weasel relatives by a pale buff patch on their throat and breast. They spend much of their time in trees pursuing red squirrels.

Black bear cubs climb trees when they sense danger. Their short claws enable them to rapidly scramble up a tree like a squirrel.

The distribution of these magnificent mammals has been reduced in recent years with the degradation of low-elevation wintering ranges.

In the high country the shrill whistle of a marmot, largest of the squirrels, is a common sound. Hoary marmots are so named for the silver cast of their fur. They live in colonies and hibernate under boulders. During the summer, marmots perch atop rocks, always on the lookout for golden eagles, wolverines, and mountain lions.

A white-tailed ptarmigan in summer plumage is mottled brown and white. This alpine grouse has feathered legs that act like snowshoes.

hibernation. Sleeping bears, however, can easily be awakened from their winter's slumber.

The range of the grizzly has drastically diminished with the spread of civilization. At once admired and feared, grizzlies are a symbol of the wilderness. Gone are the days of open garbage dumps to attract bears for the entertainment of people. Bear management within the park involves protecting both bears and people by informing visitors about precautions to take while hiking and camping in bear country.

HARDY INDIVIDUALS

Bighorn sheep move up mountainsides to summer in the high country. Rams form small groups and roam at higher elevations than ewes and lambs. With the onset of winter, males and females herd together on winter ranges. The sound of clashing horns echoes for miles as males participate in this bloodless test of strength and endurance to determine which of them will breed.

Nesting in the high country, gray-crowned rosy finches glean insects and seeds from snowbanks, while white-crowned sparrows sing from the broken tops of subalpine firs. With a continually wagging, white-edged tail, another bird—the water pipet—catches insects in wet meadows and, like the white-crowned sparrow, nests on the ground.

Also found in the high country are Clark's nutcrackers. They harvest whitebark pine cones in the fall and bury the seeds for use during the following winter and spring. Forgotten seeds from caches take root and are important in the establishment and regeneration of this tree.

The only bird in the alpine during winter is the ground-dwelling white-tailed ptarmigan, a high-elevation grouse. Along with its slow movements, the ptarmigan's mottled-brown summer feathers and white winter plumage help camouflage it from predators. The ptarmigan's feet are covered by stiff feathers that enable the bird to walk over snow. By burrowing down, the ptarmigan takes advantage of the snow's insulating quality.

Besides occasional predators on the prowl, the only mammals enduring winter in the alpine are pikas and mountain goats. Throughout the summer and fall months, pikas gather small plants and dry them on rocks for use during the winter. A five-ounce pika may store 30 pounds of dried "hay" in numerous piles about the boulder fields

The characteristic bugling of the elk, or wapiti, signals autumn, when bull elk challenge each other for females. Elk gather together for the fall rut, when males round up harems of females.

Scurrying about the boulderfields in summer, the pika is ever watchful for predators. These small rabbits, living on caches of summer-stored grasses, are active throughout the winter.

in which it lives. These rock rabbits live in colonies; they send out an "eek" of alarm with the approach of weasels, hawks, or people.

Mountain goats find year-round food in the high country in the form of grasses, sedges, mosses, and lichens. Mountain goats will travel long distances in the spring and fall to natural mineral licks to satisfy their hunger for salt. The Walton Goat Lick along Highway 89 is a natural source of salt and other minerals. Not a true goat, they are related to the European chamois. Taking shelter from ledges and rock overhangs, mountain goats endure the rigors of Glacier's winter.

The hoary marmot feeds all summer, building up a layer of fat to carry it through its winter hibernation like other squirrels.

SUGGESTED READINGS

Chadwick, Douglas. *A Beast the Color of Winter.* San Francisco: Sierra Club Books, 1983.

Gildart, Robert C. *Meet the Mammals of Waterton-Glacier International Peace Park.* West Glacier, Montana: Glacier Natural History Association, 1975.

Gildart, Robert C., and Jan Wassink. *Montana Wildlife.* Helena: Montana Magazine, Inc., 1982.

Herrero, Stephen. *Bear Attacks: Their Causes and Avoidance.* Piscataway, New Jersey: Winchester Press, 1985.

Patent, Dorothy H. *Where the Bald Eagles Gather.* New York: Clarion Books, 1984.

Man at Glacier

Like wind sweeping across a prairie, the first Native Americans left no trace of their travels in the present-day Glacier area. Place names in the park only hint at the peoples of the past: Stoney Indian Pass, and Medicine Grizzly Peak. Histories of early Native Americans in the area of Glacier include bits of stories pieced together, along with mystery and wonder of times past.

Several Indian tribes lived along the foothills of the northern Rockies. Tribes west of the Continental Divide included the Kootenai, Kalispel (Pend d'Oreille), and Flathead. Several times a year they traveled east through the mountains in the Glacier area to hunt buffalo (American bison) on the plains. These hunting parties often skirmished with Blackfeet Indians.

Today the Blackfeet Confederation includes three tribes: the Northern Blackfeet (Siksika), the Blood (Kainah), and the Piegan (Pikuni). Although the Blackfeet lived on the plains, the mountains were sites for ceremonial rituals. These people obtained food, clothing, and shelter from the buffalo they hunted. With the introduction of horses and firearms by Europeans, the Blackfeet dominated the upper Great Plains throughout much of the 1800s.

The Stoney Indians lived east of the Divide in the forested foothills at the foot of the mountains. This small tribe probably camped in the Belly River area in the northeastern corner of Glacier and the Waterton Lakes area of Canada.

FUR TRAPPERS AND TRADERS

The vast Rocky Mountain front initially presented a wild and foreign barrier to transcontinental movement. Thus the entire upper Missouri

KATHLEEN AHLENSLAGER

Towering Chief Mountain has long been a landmark for travelers along the eastern front of the mountains. The boundary between Glacier and the Blackfeet Indian Reservation cuts across the peak of Chief Mountain. Below, aspen and willows of the grasslands extend into the mountains.

River region remained essentially unexplored until after the early 1800s. The presence of hostile Blackfeet, coupled with the difficult terrain, made other routes through the Rockies more feasible. Early explorations stimulated interest in this area, especially among fur trappers and traders who stood to gain from the abundance of beaver in the streams.

The first recorded sighting of the mountains of Glacier by a white person was that of David Thompson, a Hudson Bay Company agent, in the 1780s. Another agent, Peter Fidler, traveled

With over 720 miles of maintained trails, Glacier National Park is a hiker's paradise. In Belly River country, Cosley Lake is one of several lakes in the valley below Stoney Indian Pass. Numerous mountains, lakes, and streams east of the Continental Divide are named for the various early peoples in this area.

to the eastern foot of the mountains in 1792 and attached the first place name to the Glacier area. He had named today's Chief Mountain, "King's Mountain." This same landmark is also shown on an 1806 map from the Lewis and Clark Expedition. Meriwether Lewis, on his return trip, viewed the eastern front of the mountains from about 25 miles away.

The earliest record of white men traveling through the mountains of Glacier is that of an 1810 hunting party. It included Finian MacDonald, an employee of an English trading post, two French Canadians, and several Flathead Indians.

41

The rich reflections of Mount Rockwell and Mount Sinopah in Cobalt Lake are striking. As these rugged mountains erode, loose rocks accumulate below the sheer walls and form funnel-shaped talus slopes.

Eventually several trading companies and forts were established, for several nations competed not only for beaver pelts but also for possession of the land.

THE SEARCH FOR WEALTH

A succession of surveyors, prospectors, homesteaders, and businessmen followed the early fur trappers and traders. Through the Louisiana Purchase in 1803, the United States bought from France much of the land of Glacier east of the Continental Divide. Then in 1818 an agreement between England and the United States set the 49th parallel as the boundary from the Lake of the Woods in Minnesota to the crest of the Rockies. In 1846 the boundary was extended westward to the Strait of Georgia, but it was not marked until 1874.

With the acquisition of California and the Oregon Territory by the United States, Congress authorized a survey of routes for a transcontinental railroad. Isaac I. Stevens, in charge of the survey

Beyond Two Medicine Lake, Pumpelly's Pillar points like a finger from the easternmost edge of Mount Helen. Steeple-shaped spruce and fir trees fill the slopes below.

Red buses have been traversing the Going-to-the-Sun Road almost since it opened in 1933. This 50-mile-long highway connects the east and west sides of the park. It is open only during the summer and fall months. Mount Clements straddles the Continental Divide at Logan Pass.

for a northern route, sent A. W. Tinkham in search of Marias Pass, a route used by Indians. Tinkham did not find Marias Pass but instead crossed Cut Bank Pass in 1853. In doing so, he was the first known white man to travel in the mountains of Glacier since 1810.

Sent to continue the search was John Doty. In 1854 he hiked up to the summit of Marias Pass. A southern transcontinental route was chosen, however, and interest in this area waned once again. Marias Pass was not officially discovered until almost 40 years later.

In 1889 James J. Hill, president of the Great Northern Railway, sent John F. Stevens to verify reports of this low pass through the northern Rockies. The accessibility of the Glacier area increased with the completion of Hill's transcontinental railroad over Marias Pass in 1891.

Sparked by the apparent discovery of copper and quartz outcrops east of the Continental Divide in the Many Glacier area, Montana residents pressured Congress to negotiate with the Blackfeet for the sale of this land. Controversy still surrounds the issue of whether the federal government paid $1,500,000 to buy or lease land that included the "Ceded Strip"—all of Glacier east of the Divide. In 1889 the Ceded Strip was opened to mining.

Altyn, a boomtown near present-day Many Glacier Valley, was a center for mining activity. Although population estimates for Altyn range from 300 to 1,000, no ore of any value was found there. By 1902 most of the mining activity had come to a standstill as prospectors left for more promising areas.

In 1889 a well-publicized mineral strike on the west side of today's park attracted hundreds of miners. In addition, oil strikes near Kintla Lake in 1892 and the Swiftcurrent Valley in 1902 resulted in numerous oil and mineral claims. Most of these, however, were abandoned within a year.

During this same period of mineral exploration, the seeds of land protection were sown with the introduction of a bill in 1885 to establish a forest reserve in the area of the present national park. Congress authorized the establishment of Lewis and Clark Forest Reserve in 1891.

To preserve watersheds forest rangers protected this area from unregulated public entry and wholesale forest cutting for the next ten years. In 1910 Theodore Roosevelt appointed one of his former Rough Riders, Frank Herrig, as the first forest ranger. Another forest ranger, Frank Liebig, patrolled from 1902 until 1910 a territory encompassing the whole of Glacier. He watched for fires, prevented the stealing of timber, and kept trails open and squatters out.

VISITORS WITH A VISION

The Great Northern Railroad transported westward not only miners but also homesteaders. Early families at Lake McDonald and the North Fork of the Flathead River drainage found the land impossible for farming and grazing. Wildlife was plentiful, so they maintained trap lines to support their homesteads. In addition, Milo Apgar and Charlie Howe provided "visitor services" for tourists and local miners who occasionally got off the train at Belton to visit Lake McDonald.

43

The waters of five valleys spill into Swiftcurrent Lake. On its shore, historic Many Glacier Hotel provides tired park visitors with an evening resting place and a dramatic view of Mount Gould.

Professor Lyman B. Sperry of Minnesota's Carleton College was asked to ride the new railroad and record the scenic features of the region. He became a publicist for the panoramic beauty of this land, introducing numerous people to it. Tourism had begun. James Hill promoted the attractions to encourage rail passenger traffic. Within a few years there were cabins, a hotel, a steamer, and pack trips by horse into the Lake McDonald area.

During this same time the idea of conservation of natural resources was gathering public support as Americans began to realize that minerals, forests, and water were exhaustible. One of these conservationists, George Bird Grinnell, made several trips to this region to hunt and fish. He wrote a series of articles in *Forest and Stream* magazine and a 1901 essay entitled "The Crown of the Continent" in *Century* magazine. In these writings he described the grandeur of the Glacier area and a plan for its preservation.

As a result of several years of effort by Grinnell, along with the support of Montana Congressman Charles N. Pray, President William Howard Taft signed legislation creating Glacier National Park on May 11, 1910.

HANS WENDLER

LARRY BURTON

During winter months skiers and snowshoers travel the trails of Glacier. Numbing temperatures take away the breath of visitors to the snow-covered shores of Lake McDonald.

Providing for the Public

Establishment of the new national park was not supported by everyone. Those opposed were concerned that resources would be "locked up." Providing a plan for the development of the park was one of the duties of Major William Logan, appointed superintendent of road and trail construction of Glacier.

The act enabling the establishment of Glacier included two primary objectives: preserving the park in a "state of nature" and providing for a "pleasure ground for the benefit and enjoyment of the people." Road, trail, and hotel attractions were developed and emphasized from these early days until the 1930s.

In competition with the Canadian Pacific Railway in Banff National Park in Alberta and the Northern Pacific Railway in Yellowstone, James Hill promoted the development of facilities in Glacier. His main objective was to make Glacier the "playground of the Northwest." He and his son Louis supervised the construction of several hotels, chalets, and trails within the park. In addition, a saddle-horse concession was initiated in

45

1925 with 1,000 horses carrying over 10,000 people into Glacier's backcountry every year until the 1930s.

Efforts of Montana and Alberta Rotary International clubs resulted in the establishment in 1932 of Waterton-Glacier International Peace Park—the world's first international peace park. Although separated by an international boundary and administered by two governments, the two parks are joined in name and spirit to commemorate friendship and goodwill between countries. Joint agreements between the two parks include the management of fires, bears, and search-and-rescue operations.

After the establishment of Glacier there was talk of a transmountain highway to cross the Continental Divide and connect the east and west sides of the park. Begun in 1916 and completed in 1932, the Going-to-the-Sun Road is still considered a major engineering feat. Blasted from rock at a cost of three million dollars, this scenic highway winds 52 miles over Logan Pass. Its dedication in 1933 heralded the decline of horseback sightseeing and signaled a new era of motorized travel in Glacier National Park.

Since 1927 the Prince of Wales Hotel has stood at the north end of Waterton Lake. The surrounding Waterton Lakes National Park was set aside in 1895. This Canadian park is directly north of Glacier. The international boundary crosses Waterton Lake. Glacier's highest peak is Mount Cleveland, which rises to the east of Waterton Lake. These two adjacent parks comprise Waterton-Glacier International Peace Park.

SUGGESTED READINGS

BUCHHOLTZ, C. W. *Man in Glacier.* West Glacier, Montana: Glacier Natural History Association, 1976.

GRINNELL, GEORGE B. *Blackfoot Lodge Tales.* Lincoln: University of Nebraska Press, 1962.

HOLTERMAN, JACK. *Place Names of Glacier/Waterton National Parks.* Helena, Montana: Falcon Press Publishing Co., Inc., 1985.

HOUK, ROSE. *Going-to-the-Sun: The Story of the Highway Across Glacier National Park.* Del Mar, California: Woodlands Press, 1984.

SAX, JOSEPH L. *Mountains Without Handrails: Reflections on the National Parks.* Ann Arbor: University of Michigan Press, 1980.

46

GLACIER NATIONAL PARK

Rising from the plains, the eastern front of Glacier blends into a mountain chain extending north and south as far as the eye can see. From its ice-capped peaks the "land of the shining mountains" not only shines but also sparkles like a "jewel in the crown of the continent." Descriptive phrases used by Grinnell one hundred years ago still apply to Glacier today.

Once viewed as an enormous wilderness of forested slopes and abundant wildlife, Glacier is now a wilderness island amid a region of development. Park managers today work with adjoining landowners including the Canadian government, the Blackfeet Reservation, the U.S. Forest Service, and private individuals. Issues concerning the park and its neighbors range from livestock trespass, wildlife management, and pine beetle infestation to mineral exploration, logging, and air and water pollution.

Glacier National Park is an integral part of the northern Rocky Mountain ecosystem. Conservation of Glacier's resources and processes requires management of whole ecosystems, not just parts of them. There remains for the public and park rangers the challenge of conserving Glacier National Park—where people seek self-renewal, native plants flourish, and wildlife has room to roam.

NEAL & MARY JANE MISHLER

The future of bighorn sheep and all other wild mammals, as well as bird, fish, and plant species, depends upon the wise management of their native habitats.

Inside back cover: An early September snow has settled on Dusty Star Mountain. Photo by Gary Ladd.

Back cover: Bearhat Mountain from Hidden Lake Overlook. Photo by Larry Ulrich.

Books in this series: Acadia, Alcatraz Island, Arches, Blue Ridge Parkway, Bryce Canyon, Canyon de Chelly, Cape Cod, Capitol Reef, Channel Islands, Civil War Parks, Crater Lake, Death Valley, Denali, Dinosaur, Everglades, Fort Clatsop, Gettysburg, Glacier, Glen Canyon–Lake Powell, Grand Canyon, Grand Teton, Great Smoky Mountains, Haleakala, Hawaii Volcanoes, Lake Mead–Hoover Dam, Lassen Volcanic, Lincoln Parks, Mount Rainier, Mount Rushmore, Mount St. Helens, National Park Service, National Seashores, North Cascades, Olympic, Petrified Forest, Redwood, Rocky Mountain, Scotty's Castle, Sequoia–Kings Canyon, Shenandoah, Statue of Liberty, Theodore Roosevelt, Virgin Islands, Yellowstone, Yosemite, Zion.

Published by KC Publications · Box 14883 · Las Vegas, NV 89114

Printed by Dong-A Printing Co., Ltd., Seoul, Korea
Separations by Kwangyangsa Co., Ltd.
Typography by Stanley Stillion